I Can't Believe It's Sweatshirts™

General Information

Many of the products used in this pattern book can be purchased from local craft, fabric and variety stores, or from the Annie's Attic Needlecraft Catalog (see Customer Service information on page 24).

Contents

2 Tabard Tank

4 Tres Chic

7 Casual, Cozy & Cool

12 Versatile Vest

14 Poppin' Paisleys

18 Shearling Swing

23 Stitch Guide

24 Metric Conversion Charts

Tabard Tank

SKILL LEVEL
INTERMEDIATE

FINISHED SIZE
Sweatshirt size

MATERIALS
- Red Heart Heart & Sole super fine (fingering) weight yarn (1¾ oz/213 yds/50g per skein): 2 skeins #3960 spring stripe
- Size D/3/3.25mm crochet hook or size needed to obtain gauge
- Tapestry needle
- Ladies blue sweatshirt
- Straight pins
- Marking pencil
- Liquid seam sealant

SUPER FINE 1

GAUGE
6 hdc = 1 inch

PATTERN NOTES
Chain-3 at beginning of row or round counts as first half double crochet and chain-1 unless otherwise stated.

Join with slip stitch as indicated unless otherwise stated.

Chain-2 at beginning of row or round counts as first half double crochet unless otherwise stated.

SWEATSHIRT PREPARATION
1. Remove bottom band from sweatshirt, cutting just above band.

2. Remove neckband from sweatshirt, cutting just below band.

3. Remove sleeves from sweatshirt, cutting just inside seam.

4. Lay sweatshirt flat, cut 6 inches from bottom toward armhole. Cut to round corners.

5. Measure 5 inches in from each side at bottom, draw princess lines on Front and Back (see Fig. 1).

6. Apply liquid seam sealant to cut edges.

7. Fold cut edges under ¼ inch and press in place.

8. With tapestry needle and yarn, using **double running stitch** (see Fig. 2), embroider ¼ inch outside princess lines, adding space for armhole and waistline darts as shown (see Fig. 1).

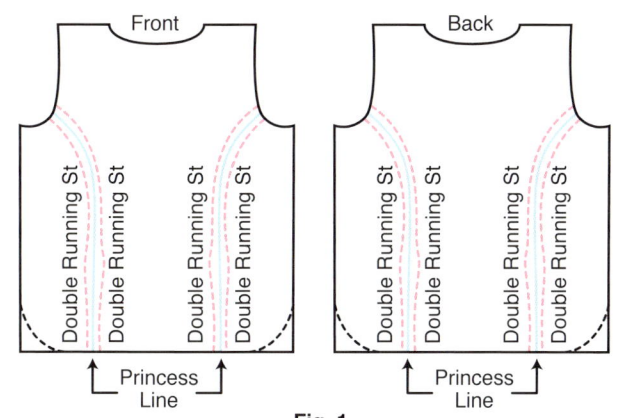

Fig. 1
Tabard Tank Diagram

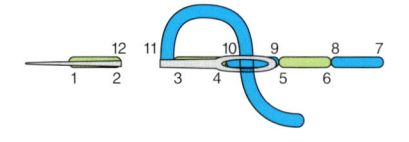

Fig. 2
Double Running Stitch

9. With tapestry needle and yarn, using **blanket stitch** (*see Fig. 3*), embroider along folded edges.

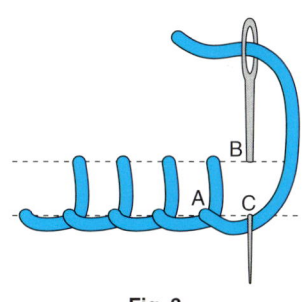

Fig. 3
Blanket Stitch

PRINCESS LINE EDGING
Folding excess to inside of sweatshirt and working in both rows of double running sts tog, sc in next double running st, evenly sp [ch 1, sc in next double running st] along princess line from 1 edge to other.

Rep for each princess line.

OUTER EDGE
Rnd 1: Working in blanket sts on WS, join with sc, evenly sp [ch 1, sc in blanket st] around edge, ch 1, **join** (*see Pattern Notes*) in beg sc, turn.

Rnd 2 (RS): Ch 1, *sc in next ch-1 sp, ch 3, sk next ch sp, rep from * around, join in beg sc, turn.

Rnd 3: **Ch 2** (*see Pattern Notes*), [sk next sc, 3 hdc in next ch-3 sp, ch 2] around, join in beg hdc. Fasten off.

INNER EDGE
Working in legs of blanket sts on RS, join with sc, evenly sp [ch 1, sc in blanket st] around, ch 1, join in beg sc. Fasten off.

NECK EDGING
Beg at center back, work Outer and Inner Edge instructions.

ARMHOLE EDGING
Beg at bottom of armhole, work Outer and Inner Edge instructions on each armhole.

BOTTOM EDGING
Beg along bottom of back, work Outer Edge instructions.

INNER EDGE
Beg along bottom of back, follow Inner Edge instructions to within 1 inch of top of side slit, hold front Outer Edging overlapping back blanket sts, [sl st in Outer Edging, ch 1, sc in blanket st, ch 1] across to top of side slit, continue with Inner Edge instructions, overlapping front Outer Edging on 2nd side.

TIES
Row 1: Join with sc in Inner Edging at side 2½ inches from top of edging, sc in same st, sc in next st, turn.

Row 2: Ch 1, sc in each sc, turn.

Next rows: Rep row 2 until Tie measures 6 inches. At end of last row, fasten off.

Rep on opposite outer edging.

Rep on 2nd side.

POCKET
MAKE 2.
Row 1: Ch 3 (see Pattern Notes), (hdc, ch 3, 2 hdc) in 3rd ch from hook, turn.

Row 2: Ch 3, sk next hdc, (2 hdc, ch 3, 2 hdc) in next ch-3 sp, ch 1, hdc in last hdc, turn.

Row 3: Ch 2, hdc in first ch-1 sp, ch 1, sk next 2 hdc, (2 hdc, ch 3, 2 hdc) in next ch-3 sp, ch 1, sk next 2 hdc, 2 hdc in last ch-1 sp, turn.

Row 4: Ch 3, *2 hdc in next ch-1 sp, ch 1*, (2 hdc, ch 3, 2 hdc) in next ch-3 sp, ch 1, rep between *, hdc in last hdc, turn.

Row 5: Ch 2, hdc in first ch-1 sp, *ch 1, 2 hdc in next ch-1 sp*, ch 1, (2 hdc, ch 3, 2 hdc) in next ch-3 sp, rep between *, ch 1, hdc in next ch-1 sp, hdc in last st, turn.

Row 6: Ch 3, *2 hdc in next ch-1 sp, ch 1*, rep between * across to corner, (2 hdc, ch 3, 2 hdc) in next ch-3 sp, ch 1, rep between * across, hdc in last hdc, turn.

Row 7: Ch 2, hdc in first ch-1 sp, *ch 1, 2 hdc in next ch-1 sp*, rep between * across to corner, ch 1, (2 hdc, ch 3, 2 hdc) in next ch-3 sp, rep between * across to last ch-1 sp, ch 1, hdc in last ch-1 sp, hdc in last st, turn.

Rows 8–17: [Rep rows 6 and 7 alternately] 5 times.

Row 18: Rep row 6.

Last rnd: Ch 1, evenly sp (sc, ch 1) around all edges, join in beg sc. Fasten off.

FINISHING
With tapestry needle and yarn, sew Pockets in place as shown in photo. ■

Tres Chic

SKILL LEVEL
INTERMEDIATE

FINISHED SIZE
Sweatshirt size

MATERIALS
- Red Heart LusterSheen fine (sport) weight yarn (4 oz/335 yds/113g per skein):
    1 skein each #0001 white and #0002 black
- Size F/5/3.75mm crochet hook or size needed to obtain gauge
- Tapestry needle
- Sewing needle
- Black sewing thread
- Ladies white sweatshirt
- Ladies black sweatshirt: 2
- Elastic:
    To fit around waist plus 2 inches and ½ inch less than width of bottom band of black sweatshirt
- Straight pins
- Marking pencil
- Liquid seam sealant

2 FINE

GAUGE
16 dc = 4 inches

PATTERN NOTES
Double crochet stitches should be dense, but should not ruffle.

Wrong side of double crochet is right side of edging when folded down over cut edge.

Chain-3 at beginning of row or round counts as first double crochet unless otherwise stated.

Join with slip stitch as indicated unless otherwise stated.

JACKET SWEATSHIRT PREPARATION

1. Remove bottom band from 1 white and 1 black sweatshirt, cutting just above band.

2. Remove neckband from each sweatshirt, cutting just below band.

3. Remove band from each sleeve, cutting just above band.

4. Lay each sweatshirt flat, cut down center front.

5. Measure 1 inch from each front edge and cut. Cut to round corners at top and bottom.

6. Apply liquid seam sealant to cut edges.

7. With WS tog and cut edges even, pin both sweatshirts tog.

8. With tapestry needle and yarn *(either color)*, using **double running stitch** *(see Fig. 1)*, embroider ¼ inch from cut edges.

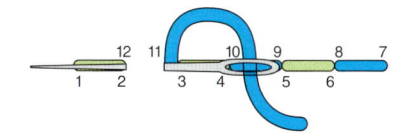

Fig. 1
Double Running Stitch

SKIRT SWEATSHIRT PREPARATION

1. Remove each sleeve from sweatshirt, cutting just inside seams.

2. Cut through front and back from side to side just below front neck band. Cut to round corners.

3. Carefully cut a slit through inside of bottom band *(now waistband)* to insert elastic.

4. Apply liquid seam sealant to cut edges.

5. With tapestry needle and yarn, using double running stitch, embroider ¼ inch from cut edge.

JACKET
OUTER EDGES
FIRST SIDE

Rnd 1: Working in running sts on black side, **join** *(see Pattern Notes)* white in st at center of back neck, **ch 3** *(see Pattern Notes)*, evenly sp dc along edge with right side of dc facing edge of sweatshirt, join in 3rd ch of beg ch-3, **turn**.

Rnd 2: Ch 1, sc in each dc around, join in beg sc. Fasten off.

SIDE 2

Rnds 1 & 2: On white side with black yarn, follow instructions for First Side, **do not fasten off** at end of rnd 2, turn.

Rnd 3: Working in corresponding sts of both sides tog, sl st in **back lp** *(see Stitch Guide)* of each sc around, join in beg sl st, turn.

Rnd 4: Ch 1, working over sl sts of last rnd, sc in first st, [ch 5, sk next 3 sts, sc in next st] around, ch 5, sk last 3 sts, join in beg sc. Fasten off.

Rnd 5: Sk 1 st from first sc of previous rnd, join white with sc over next sl st, [ch 5, sk next 3 sts, working behind ch-5 of previous rnd, sc over next sl st, ch 5, sk next 3 sts, working in front of ch-5 of previous rnd, sc over next sl st] around, ch 5, sk last 3 sts, join in beg sc. Fasten off.

Work Outer Edges around each Sleeve beg at seam.

SKIRT
OUTSIDE EDGING

Rnd 1: Working in running sts on RS, join white in any st at top of either side slit, ch 3, evenly sp dc along edge with RS of dc facing edge of sweatshirt, join in 3rd ch of beg ch-3, turn.

Rnd 2: Ch 1, sc in each dc around, join in beg sc. Fasten off.

INSIDE EDGING

Rnds 1 & 2: On WS with black, follow instructions for Outside Edging, do not fasten of at end of row 2, turn.

Rnd 3: Working in corresponding sts of Outside and Inside Edgings tog, ch 1, sl st in back lps of each sc around, join in beg sc, turn.

Rnd 4: Ch 1, working over sl sts of last rnd, sc in next st, [ch 5, sk next 3 sts, sc in next st] around, ch 5, sk last 3 sts, join in beg sc. Fasten off.

Rnd 5: Sk 1 st from first sc of previous rnd, join white yarn with sc over next sl st, [ch 5, sk next 3 sts, working behind ch-5 of previous rnd, sc in next st, ch 5, sk next 3 sts, working in front of ch-5 of previous rnd, sc in next st] around, ch 5, sk last 3 sts, join in beg sc. Fasten off.

LARGE FLOWERS
MAKE 3 WHITE AND 2 BLACK.

Ch 2, sc in 2nd ch from hook [ch 7, sc in same ch as first sc] 5 times, ch 7, join in beg sc. Leaving long end, fasten off.

SMALL FLOWERS
MAKE 6 WHITE AND 4 BLACK.

Ch 2, sc in 2nd ch from hook [ch 5, sc in same ch as first sc] 5 times, ch 5, join in beg sc. Leaving long end, fasten off.

FINISHING

Using long ends, sew Flowers to Jacket and Skirt as shown in photo.

Insert elastic in opening in Waistband, overlap edges 1 inch, sew tog. Sew opening closed. ∎

Casual, Cozy & Cool

SKILL LEVEL
INTERMEDIATE

FINISHED SIZE
Sweatshirt size

MATERIALS
- NaturallyCaron.com Country medium (worsted) weight yarn (3 oz/185 yds/85g per skein): 4 skeins #0008 silver service
- Size I/9/5.5mm crochet hook or size needed to obtain gauge
- Tapestry needle
- Sewing needle
- Silver and gray sewing thread
- Ladies sweatshirt
- Ladies sweatpants
- ¾-inch buttons: 5
- Straight pins
- Marking pencil
- Liquid seam sealant

GAUGE
4 dc = 1 inch; 2 rows = 1½ inches

PATTERN NOTES
Chain-3 at beginning of row or round counts as first double crochet unless otherwise stated.

Chain-4 at beginning of row or round counts as first double crochet and chain-1 unless otherwise stated.

Chain-5 at beginning of row or round counts as first double crochet and chain-2 unless otherwise stated.

Chain-6 at beginning of row or round counts as first double crochet and chain-3 unless otherwise stated.

Chain-1, join with double crochet counts as last chain-3 space.

When working blanket stitches and instructions call for skipped stitches, skip 3 or 4 blanket stitches as needed to keep work even.

Do not fasten off after insets before pants and sleeves are completed; follow instructions for joining to blanket stitches, do not fasten off, then follow instructions for trim.

For top, fasten off after joining left front and both back insets to blanket stitches. Right front inset should be completed last, do not fasten off, then follow instructions for joining and trim.

Chain spaces of front trim are used as buttonholes.

SPECIAL STITCHES
V-stitch (V-st): (Dc, ch 3, dc) in place indicated.

Extended single crochet (ext sc): Insert hook in st, yo, pull through 1 lp on hook, yo, pull through all lps on hook.

TOP SWEATSHIRT PREPARATION
1. Remove bottom band from sweatshirt, cutting just above band.

2. Remove band from around each sleeve, cutting just above band.

3. Make 10-inch cut on each sleeve from bottom up, directly opposite sleeve seams.

4. Lay sweatshirt flat, cut down center front.

5. Keep sweatshirt flat, mark point on each side beg 4½ inches from center front and 8 inches from bottom. Draw vertical line from each point to bottom. At bottom, mark point 2 inches to the left and 2 inches to right of each vertical line, forming triangles. Cutting through both front and back, cut out triangles (see Fig. 1).

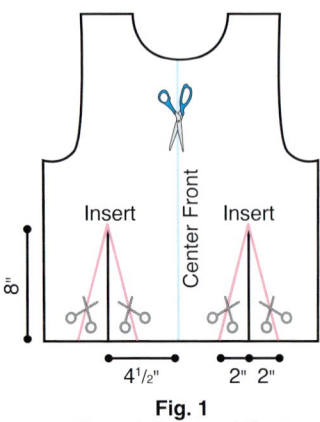

Fig. 1
Casual, Cozy and Cool Diagram

6. Apply liquid seam sealant to cut edges.

7. Fold cut edges under ¼ inch, tapering to nothing on sleeve slashes and front and back cut-outs, and press in place.

8. With tapestry needle and yarn, using **blanket stitch** (see Fig. 2), embroider along edges. Leave 3¾ inches from neck down on each front unstitched.

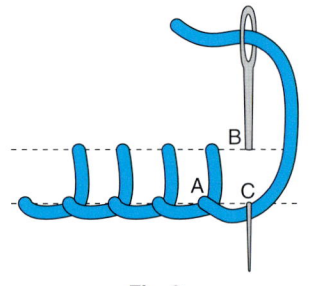

Fig. 2
Blanket Stitch

SWEAT PANTS PREPARATION
1. Lay sweatpants flat, cut 12½ inches up from hem along outside seam on each leg.

2. Apply liquid seam sealant to cut edges.

3. Fold under ¼ inch on cut edge, tapering to nothing at top of slit and press in place.

4. With tapestry needle, using blanket stitch (see Fig. 2), embroider along edges of slit and hem.

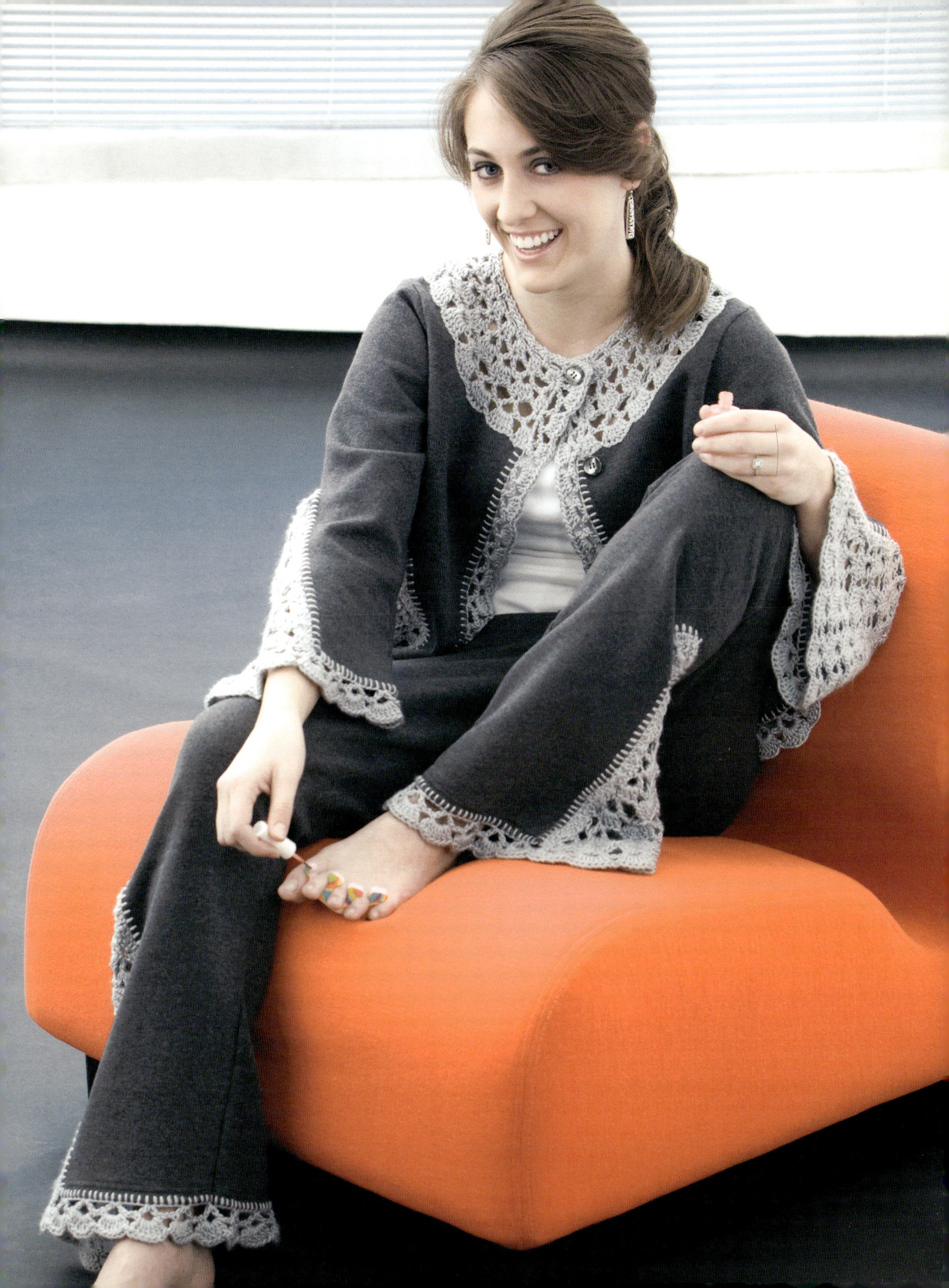

YOKE

Measure neckband. Instructions provide for first row which measures 19 inches. If measurement differs by a fraction of an inch, follow instructions as stated. If there is a difference of 1 or more inches, add or subtract 3 chains for each inch.

Row 1: (RS): Ch 76, 2 dc in 4th ch from hook (*first 3 chs count as first dc*), [sk next 2 chs, 3 dc in next ch] across, turn. *(75 dc)*

Row 2: Ch 4 (*see Pattern Notes*), dc in same st, [ch 1, sk next 4 dc, (dc, ch 2, dc) in center dc of next 3-dc group] across to last st, ch 1, (dc, ch 1, dc) in last dc, turn. *(50 dc)*

Row 3: Ch 3 (*see Pattern Notes*), 2 dc in first ch-1 sp, [ch 1, 5 dc in next ch-2 sp] across, ch 1, 2 dc in last ch-1 sp, dc in last dc, turn. *(121 dc)*

Row 4: Ch 5 (*see Pattern Notes*), dc in same st, *ch 1, **V-st** (*see Special Stitches*) in center st of next 5-dc group, rep from * across, ending with ch 1, (dc, ch 2, dc) in last st, turn. *(50 dc)*

Row 5: Ch 3, 3 dc in first ch-2 sp, [ch 1, 6 dc in next ch-3 sp] across, ch 1, 3 dc in next ch-2 sp, dc in last dc, turn. Fasten off. *(146 dc)*

Pin WS of last row of Yoke to RS of sweatshirt 4 inches from top of neckband (*RS of both should face up*). With sewing needle and silver thread, sew Yoke to sweatshirt securely.

Carefully cut away sweatshirt ¼ inch above stitching. Apply liquid seam sealant to cut edge.

INSETS
TOP: MAKE 4 WORKING INSTRUCTIONS ROWS 1–11.
SLEEVES: MAKE 2 WORKING INSTRUCTIONS ROWS 1–15.
PANTS: MAKE 2 WORKING INSTRUCTIONS ROWS 1–19.

Row 1 (RS): Ch 5, sl st in first ch to form ring, ch 4, (3 dc, ch 1, dc) in ring, turn. *(5 dc)*

Row 2: Ch 4, sk next ch-1 sp and next dc, (dc, ch 2, dc) in next dc, ch 1, dc in last dc, turn. *(4 dc)*

Row 3: Ch 4, 5 dc in next ch-2 sp, ch 1, dc in last dc, turn. *(7 dc)*

Row 4: Ch 4, dc in same dc, ch 1, sk next 2 dc, (dc, ch 2, dc) in next dc, ch 1, (dc, ch 1, dc) in last dc, turn. *(6 dc)*

Row 5: Ch 3, 2 dc in first ch-1 sp, ch 1, 5 dc in next ch-2 sp, ch 1, 2 dc in last ch-1 sp, dc in last dc, turn. *(11 dc)*

Row 6: Ch 5, dc in same dc, ch 1, sk next 4 dc, V-st in next dc, ch 1, sk next 4 dc, (dc, ch 2, dc) in last dc, turn. *(6 dc)*

Row 7: Ch 3, 3 dc in first ch-2 sp, ch 1, 7 dc in next ch-3 sp, ch 1, 3 dc in next ch-2 sp, dc in last dc, turn. *(15 dc)*

Row 8: Ch 6, dc in same dc, *ch 2, sk next 6 dc, V-st in next dc, rep from * across, turn. *(6 dc)*

Row 9: Ch 3, 4 dc in first ch-3 sp, ch 1, 7 dc in next ch-3 sp, ch 1, 4 dc in last ch-3 sp, dc in last dc, turn. *(17 dc)*

Row 10: Ch 5, sk next 2 dc, (dc, ch 2, dc) in next dc, sk next 5 dc, V-st in next dc, sk next 5 dc, (dc, ch 2, dc) in next dc, ch 2, dc in last dc, turn. *(8 dc)*

Row 11: Ch 4, sk next ch-2 sp, *5 dc in next ch-2 sp, ch 1*, 7 dc in next ch-3 sp, ch 1, rep between * once, dc in last dc, turn. *(19 dc)*

End here for Top.

Row 12: Ch 5, dc in same dc, ch 2, sk next 2 dc, *[V-st in next dc, ch 2*, sk next 5 dc] twice, rep between * once, (dc, ch 2, dc) in last dc, turn. *(10 dc)*

Row 13: Ch 3, 3 dc in first ch-2 sp, [ch 1, 7 dc in next ch-3 sp] across to next ch-2 sp, ch 1, 3 dc in ch-2 sp, dc in last st, turn. *(29 dc)*

Row 14: Rep row 8. *(10 dc)*

Row 15: Ch 3, 4 dc in first ch-3 sp, [ch 1, 7 dc in next ch-3 sp] 3 times, ch 1, 4 dc in last ch-3 sp, dc in last dc, turn. *(31 dc)*

End here for Sleeves.

Row 16: Ch 5, sk first 2 dc, *(dc, ch 2, dc) in next dc, ch 2*, sk next 5 sts, [**V-st in next dc, ch 2**, sk next 6 dc] twice, rep between ** once, sk next 5 dc, rep between * once, dc in last dc, turn. *(12 dc)*

Row 17: Ch 4, sk next ch-2 sp, *5 dc in next ch-2 sp, ch 1*, [7 dc in next ch-3 sp, ch 1] 3 times, rep between * once, dc in last dc, turn. *(33 dc)*

Row 18: Ch 5, dc in same dc, ch 2, sk next 2 dc, *V-st in next dc, ch 2*, sk next 5 dc, [rep between * once, sk next 6 dc] twice, rep between * once, sk next 5 dc, rep between * once, (dc, ch 2, dc) in last dc, turn. *(14 dc)*

Row 19: Rep row 13. *(43 dc)*

JOINING INSETS TO BLANKET STITCHES
Holding pieces with WS tog and working evenly in blanket stitches and ends of rows, ch 1, sl st in first blanket st, [ch 2, sl st in end of row, ch 1, sl st in blanket st] around Inset, turn to complete Trim. Rep for each Inset.

TRIM
OUTER JACKET EDGES
Rnd 1: Working on WS, ch 5, working steps to complete this rnd:

A. [V-st in next st, ch 2, sk 3 or 4 blanket sts] across to Inset;

B. Sk joining row, V-st in next dc, ch 2, sk next 3 sts, V-st in next dc, [ch 2, sk next 6 sts, V-st in next dc] twice, ch 2, sk next 3 sts, V-st in next dc, ch 2, sk joining row;

C. [Rep steps A and B alternately] twice, rep step A, V-st in last blanket st at corner;

D. Ch 2, working in blanket sts and ends of rows of Yoke, rep step A across to top;

E. Working on opposite side of starting ch, V-st in first ch, [ch 3, sc in next ch sp] across, ch 3, V-st in last ch;

F. Working in ends of rows of Yoke and blanket sts, rep step A across to next corner,

G. V-st in last blanket st at corner, ch 2, rep step A, [ch 2, sk next 5 sts, V-st in next dc] twice, ch 2, sk next 2 sts, dc in same st as beg ch-5, **ch 1, dc in 3rd ch of beg ch-5** *(see Pattern Notes)*, turn.

Rnd 2: Ch 3, 3 dc in same sp, *ch 1, 7 dc in next ch-3 sp*, rep between * to corner, ◊4 dc in next ch-3 sp, 3 dc in next ch-2 sp, 4 dc in next ch-3 sp◊, [ch 1, 5 dc in next ch-3 sp] across to corner, dc in last V-st, 3 sc around dc just made, 3 sc in each ch-3 sp along neckline, 3 sc in corner V-st, 3 ext sc *(see Special Stitches)*, rep between * across to corner, rep between ◊ once, rep between * across bottom, ending with 3 dc in first ch-3 sp, sl st in first dc. Fasten off.

TRIM
SLEEVES AND PANTS
Rnd 1: Working on WS, ch 5, *sk 3 or 4 blanket sts, V-st in next st, ch 2, rep from * across to Inset, sk joining row, V-st in next dc, ch 2, [sk next 6 sts, V-st in next st, ch 2] across Inset, sk next 6 sts, dc in same st as beg ch-5, ch 1, dc in 3rd ch of beg ch-5 dc, turn.

Rnd 2: Ch 3, 3 dc in same sp, [ch 1, 7 dc in next ch-3 sp] around, ending 3 dc in first ch-3 sp, join with sl st in 3rd ch of beg ch-3. Fasten off.

Work Trim on bottom of both Sleeves and on bottom of both Pant legs.

FINISHING
Using ch-1 sps of Right Front as buttonholes, sew buttons in place on Left Front. ■

Versatile Vest

SKILL LEVEL

INTERMEDIATE

FINISHED SIZE
Sweatshirt size

MATERIALS
- Caron Simply Soft Paints medium (worsted) weight yarn (4 oz/200 yds/113g per ball):
    1 ball #0006 oceana
- Size J/10/6mm crochet hook or size needed to obtain gauge
- Tapestry needle
- Sewing needle
- Navy and turquoise sewing thread
- ½-inch shank buttons:
    4 each navy and turquoise
- Ladies sweatshirts:
    1 each navy and turquoise
- Straight pins
- Marking pencil
- Liquid seam sealant

GAUGE
1 pattern rep = 1 inch

PATTERN NOTES
More than one crochet stitch may be placed in one blanket stitch, as needed for even spacing.

Chain-5 spaces on fronts serve as buttonholes.

SWEATSHIRT PREPARATION
1. Remove bottom from each sweatshirt, cutting 2 inches above band.
2. Remove neckband from each sweatshirt, cutting just below band.
3. Remove sleeves from each sweatshirt, cutting just inside seam.
4. Lay each sweatshirt flat, cut down center front.
5. Apply liquid seam sealant to cut edges.
6. Fold cut edges under ¼ inch and press in place.
7. Pin sweatshirts with WS tog.
8. With tapestry needle and yarn, using **blanket stitch** *(see Fig. 1)*, embroider along folded edges.

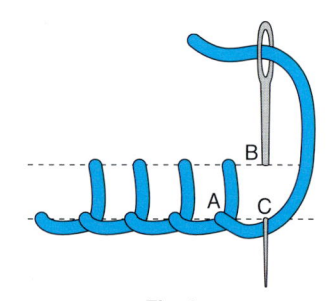

Fig. 1
Blanket Stitch

9. Measure 6 inches down from neckline, fold fronts back to form lapels.

OUTER EDGING
Working in blanket sts on navy side, join with sl st at bottom of left lapel, ◊[sc in next st, ch 1, dc in next st, ch 5, sl st in dc just made, ch 1, sc in next st, sl st in next st] 4 times◊, *sc in next st, ch 1, dc in next st, ch 3, sl st in dc just made, ch 1, sc in next st**, sl st in next st, rep from * evenly sp around to right front, rep between ◊ below right lapel, rep from * evenly sp around, ending last rep at **, join with sl st in beg sl st. Fasten off.

ARMHOLE EDGING
Working in blanket sts on navy side, join with sl st at bottom of armhole, *sc in next st, ch 1, dc

in next st, ch 3, sl st in dc just made, ch 1, sc in next st**, sl st in next st, rep from * evenly sp around armhole, ending last rep at **, join with sl st in beg sl st. Fasten off.

Rep for 2nd armhole.

FINISHING
With sewing needle and matching thread, place navy buttons on navy left front, matching buttonholes on right front, sew in place. Rep with turquoise thread and buttons on turquoise left front. ∎

Poppin' Paisleys

SKILL LEVEL
INTERMEDIATE

FINISHED SIZE
Sweatshirt size

MATERIALS
- Caron Simply Soft Paints medium (worsted) weight yarn (4 oz/200 yds/113g per ball):
    1 ball #0002 rose garden
- Size J/10/6mm crochet hook or size needed to obtain gauge
- Tapestry needle
- Sewing needle
- Pink sewing thread
- Ladies sweatshirts:
    1 each green and pink
- Pink separating zipper: length of sweatshirt excluding neck band
- Straight pins
- Marking pencil
- Liquid seam sealant

GAUGE
(Sl st, ch 1) 3 times = 1 inch; 4 rows = 1 inch

PATTERN NOTES
More than one crochet stitch may be placed in one embroidery stitch, as needed for even spacing.

Front edging will rise when zipper is closed to match paisley edging.

SWEATSHIRT PREPARATION

1. Remove neckband from green sweatshirt, cutting just below band.

2. Lay each sweatshirt flat, cut across front and back 2 inches below armholes.

3. Lay top of green sweatshirt flat, cut down center front.

4. Lay bottom of pink sweatshirt flat, cut down center front.

5. Using paisley full-size pattern pieces (see Fig. 1, page 16), cut 2 of each paisley from top of pink sweatshirt.

6. Apply liquid seam sealant to cut edges.

7. Fold cut edges of green top and pink bottom under ¼ inch and press in place.

8. Pin paisley pieces to green top as shown (see Fig. 2, Page 17).

9. With tapestry needle and yarn, using **double running stitch** (see Fig. 3), embroider ⅛ inch inside edge of paisley and just outside edge of paisley.

10. With tapestry needle and yarn, using **blanket stitch** (see Fig. 4), embroider along folded edges.

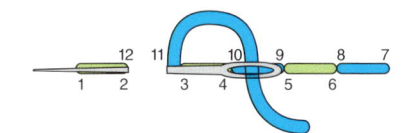

Fig. 3
Double Running Stitch

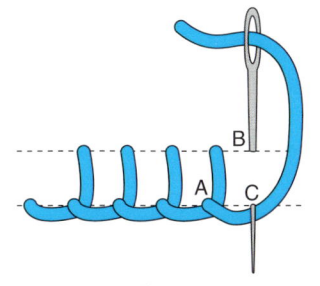

Fig. 4
Blanket Stitch

JOINING TOP AND BOTTOM

Working on RS bottom of green and WS top of pink, join yarn with sl st in first blanket st of pink sweatshirt, [ch 1, sl st in blanket st of green sweatshirt, ch 1, sl st in blanket st of pink sweatshirt] across. Fasten off.

NECK TRIM

Row 1: On RS, join with sl st in first blanket st of top of right front, [ch 1, sl st in next blanket st] across to opposite side, turn.

Rows 2 & 3: [Ch 1, sl st in next ch-1 sp] across, turn. At end of last row, fasten off.

Large
Pattern Piece A
Cut 2

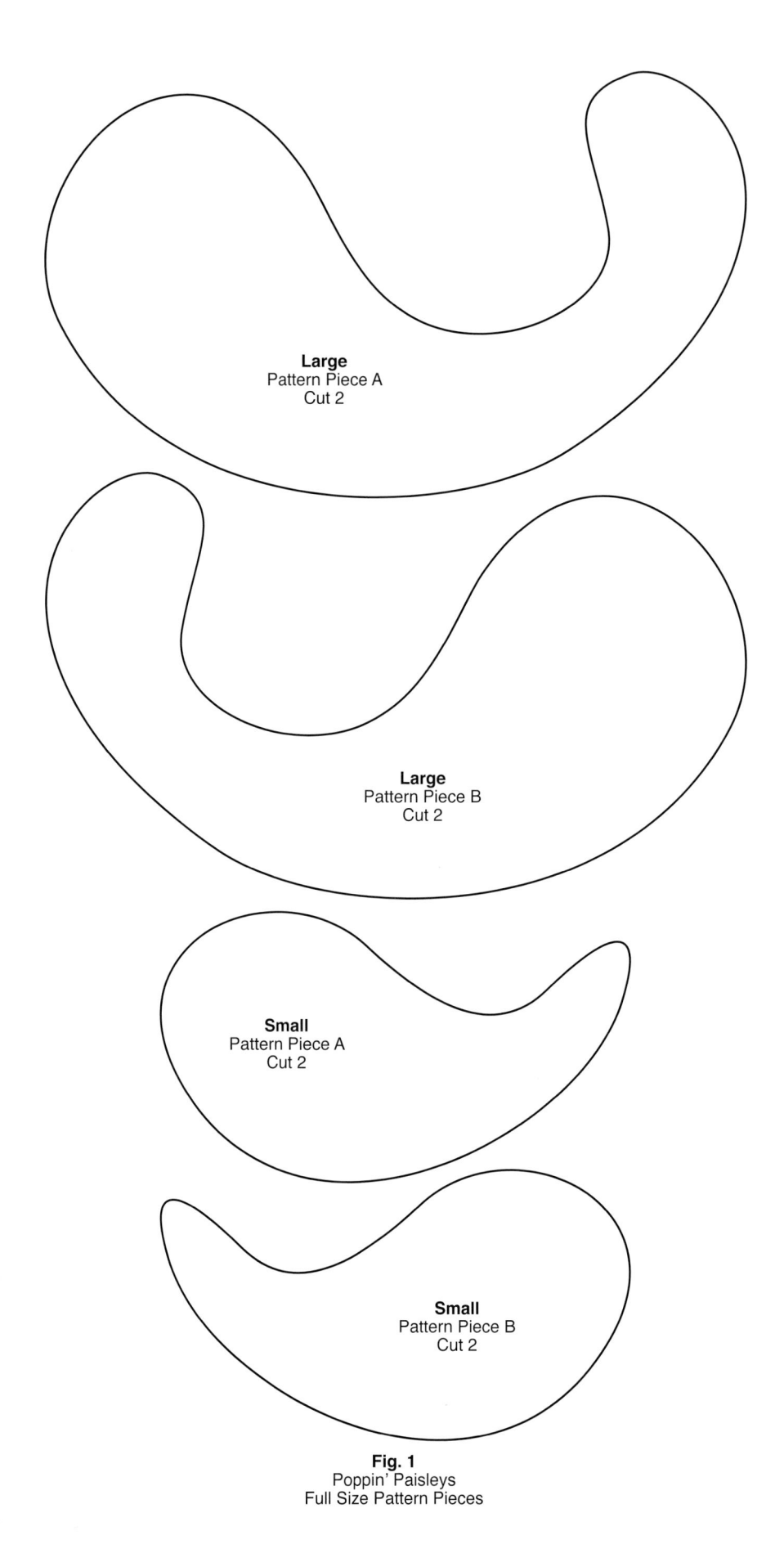

Large
Pattern Piece B
Cut 2

Small
Pattern Piece A
Cut 2

Small
Pattern Piece B
Cut 2

Fig. 1
Poppin' Paisleys
Full Size Pattern Pieces

FRONT & NECK EDGING

Row 1: With RS facing, join with sl st in first blanket st at right bottom front, [ch 1, sl st in next blanket st] across to Neck Trim, working in ends of rows, [ch 1, sl st in end of next st] twice, [ch 1, sl st in next ch sp] across Neck Trim, work in ends of rows of Neck Trim, [ch 1, sl st in end of next row] twice, working down front edge, [ch 1, sl st in next blanket st] across, turn.

Row 2: [Ch 1, sl st in next ch sp] across. Fasten off.

PAISLEY EDGING

Join with sl st in any double running st in outer row, [ch 1, sl st in double running st in inner row, ch 1, sl st in double running st in outer row] around, sl st in first st of double running st. Fasten off.

Rep for each paisley.

FINISHING

Center zipper tape over folded edges of sweatshirt *(not crochet edging)*. With sewing needle and matching thread, sew in place. ∎

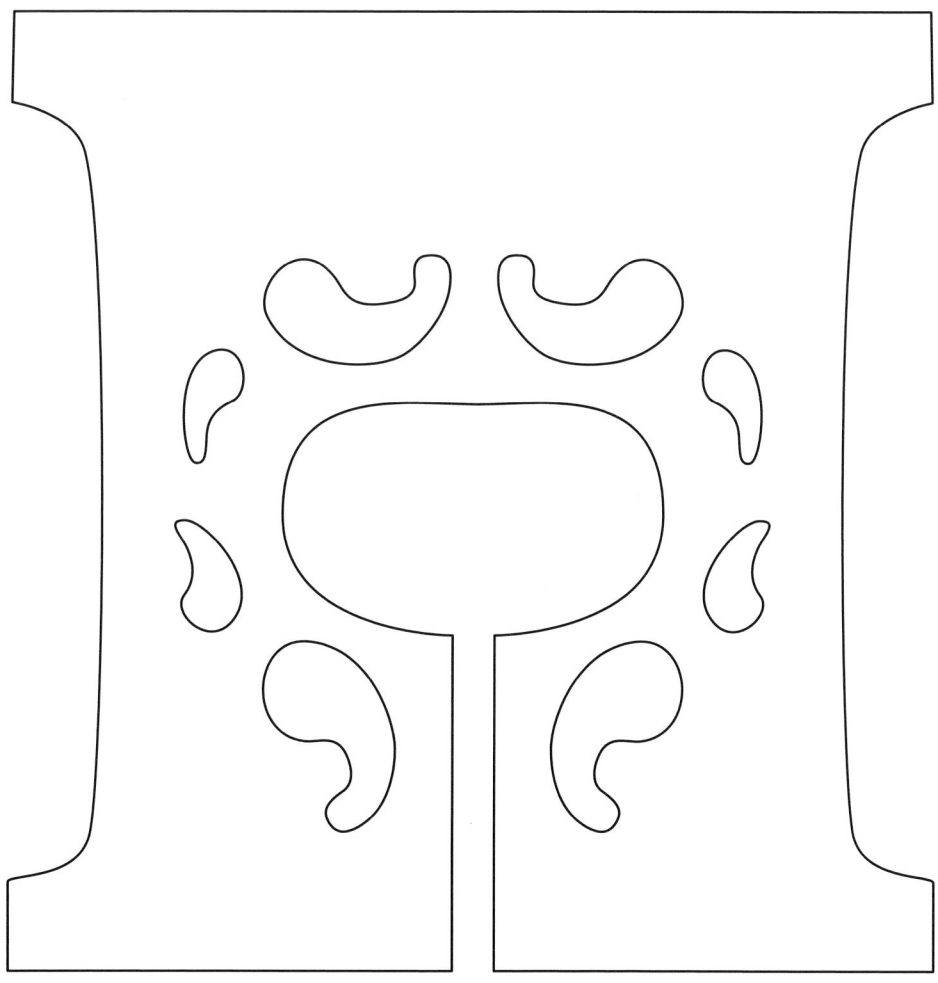

Fig. 2
Poppin' Paisleys
Placement Diagram

Shearling Swing

SKILL LEVEL
INTERMEDIATE

FINISHED SIZE
Sweatshirt size

MATERIALS
- NaturallyCaron.com Country medium (worsted) weight yarn (3 oz/185 yds/85g per skein): 3 skeins #0007 naturally
- Size H/8/5mm crochet hook or size needed to obtain gauge
- Tapestry needle
- Sewing needle
- Brown sewing thread
- Ladies sweatshirt
- Separating zipper: 8 inches less than length of sweatshirt between neckband and bottom band
- Straight pins
- Marking pencil
- Liquid seam sealant

4 MEDIUM

GAUGE
(Sc, ch 1) 8 times = 3 inches; 9 rows = 2 inches

PATTERN NOTES
Chain-3 at beginning of row or round counts as first double crochet unless otherwise stated.

Chain-5 at beginning of row or round counts as first double crochet and chain-2 unless otherwise stated.

Join with slip stitch as indicated unless otherwise stated.

SWEATSHIRT PREPARATION

1. Remove bottom band from sweatshirt, cutting just above band.

2. Remove neckband from sweatshirt, cutting just below band.

3. Remove band from each sleeve, cutting just above band.

4. Lay sweatshirt flat, cut down center front, cut 12 inches from bottom up at center back, cut 4 inches from bottom up at each side.

5. Measure 2 inches in from center front and 6½ inches up from bottom. Mark 6-inch pocket openings (see Fig. 1). Rep on rem front.

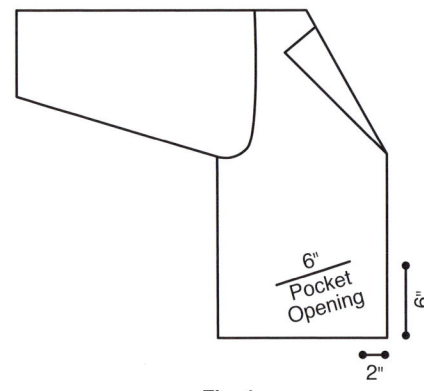

Fig. 1
Shearling Swing

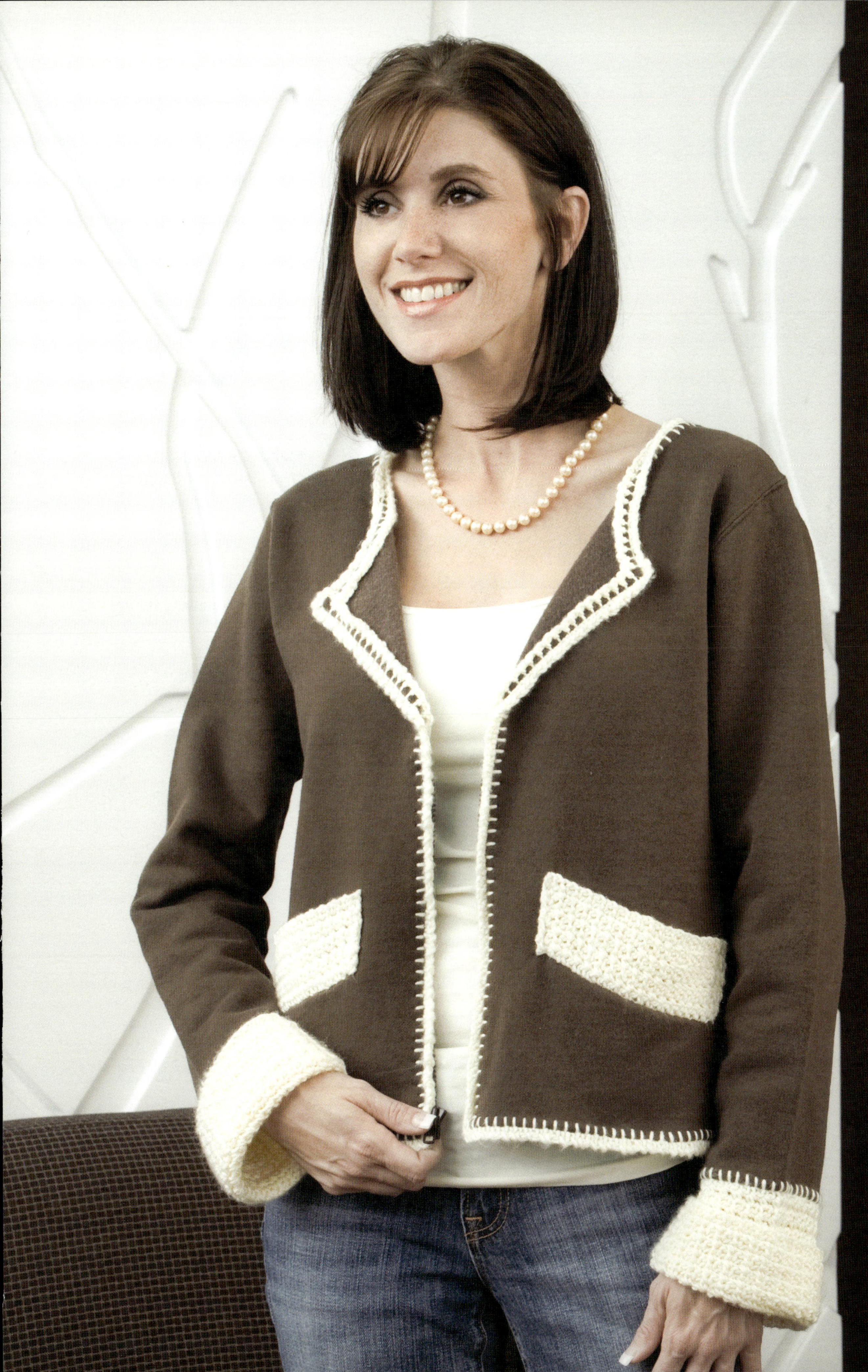

6. With tapestry needle and yarn, using **double running stitch** (see Fig. 2), embroider ⅛ inch around pocket mark and carefully slash opening between rows of stitching.

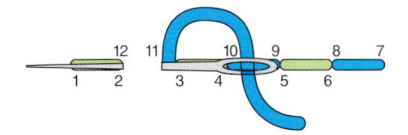

Fig. 2
Double Running Stitch

7. Apply liquid seam sealant to cut edges.

8. Fold cut edges under ¼ inch and press in place.

9. With tapestry needle and yarn, using **blanket stitch** (see Fig. 3), embroider along folded edges.

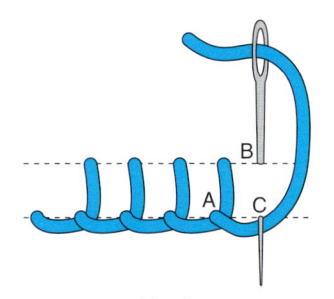

Fig. 3
Blanket Stitch

10. Measure 6 inches down from neckline, fold fronts back to form lapels.

BACK PLEAT

Row 1: Ch 5, sl st in first ch to form ring, ch 1, (sc, ch 3, sc) in ring, turn. *(2 sc)*

Row 2 (RS): Ch 3 *(see Pattern Notes)*, dc in same sc, ch 2, sc in next ch-3 sp, ch 2, 2 dc in last sc, turn. *(1 sc, 4 dc)*

Row 3: Ch 1, 2 sc in first dc, sc in next dc, ch 3, sc in next dc, 2 sc in last dc, turn. *(6 sc)*

Row 4: Ch 3, dc in each of next 2 sc, ch 2, sc in ch-3 sp, ch 2, dc in each of next 3 sc, turn. *(1 sc, 6 dc)*

Row 5: Ch 3, sc in same st, sc in each of next 2 dc, ch 3, sc in each of next 2 dc, (sc, ch 1, dc) in last st, turn.

Row 6: Ch 1, sc in first dc, [ch 2, dc in each of next 3 sc, ch 2, sc in next ch-3 sp] twice, turn. *(3 sc, 6 dc)*

Row 7: *Ch 5, sc in each of next 3 dc, rep from * across, ch 2, dc in last sc, turn. *(2 dc, 6 sc)*

Row 8: Ch 5 *(see Pattern Notes)*, *sc in next ch sp, ch 2**, dc in each of next 3 sc, ch 2, rep from * across, ending last rep at **, dc in last sc, turn. *(3 sc, 8 dc)*

Row 9: Ch 1, sc in first dc, [ch 5, sc in each of next 3 dc] across, ch 5, sc in last dc, turn. *(8 sc)*

Row 10: Ch 3, dc in same sc, *ch 2, sc in next ch-5 sp, ch 2**, dc in each of next 3 sc, rep from * across, ending last rep at **, 2 dc in last sc, turn. *(3 sc, 10 dc)*

Row 11: Ch 1, sc in each of first 2 dc, [ch 5, sc in each of next 3 dc] across, ch 5, sc in each of last 2 dc, turn. *(10 sc)*

Row 12: Ch 3, dc in same st, dc in next sc, *ch 2, sc in next ch-5 sp, ch 2**, dc in each of next 3 sc, rep from * across, ending last rep at **, dc in next sc, 2 dc in last sc, turn. *(3 sc, 12 dc)*

Row 13: Ch 5, sc in same st, sc in each of next 2 dc, [ch 5, sc in each of next 3 dc] across to last 3 sts, ch 5, sc in each of next 2 sts, (sc, ch 2, dc) in last st, turn. *(2 dc, 12 sc)*

Rows 14–18: Rep rows 8–12. *(5 sc, 18 dc at end of last row)*

Row 19: Ch 1, sc in each of first 3 dc, [ch 6, sc in each of next 3 dc] across, turn. *(18 sc)*

Row 20: Ch 3, dc in each of next 2 sc, [ch 3, sc in next ch sp, ch 3, dc in each of next 3 sc] across, turn. *(5 sc, 18 dc)*

Row 21: Ch 1, sc in each of first 3 dc, [ch 6, sc in each of next 3 dc] across, turn. *(18 sc)*

Row 22: Ch 3, dc in each of next 2 sc, [ch 4, sc in next ch sp, ch 4, dc in each of next 3 sc] across, turn. *(5 sc, 18 dc)*

Row 23: Ch 1, sc in each of first 3 dc, [ch 7, sc in each of next 3 dc] across, turn. *(18 sc)*

Row 24: Rep row 22.

Row 25: Ch 1, sc in each of first 3 dc, [ch 8, sc in each of next 3 dc] across, turn. *(18 sc)*

Row 26: Ch 3, *2 dc in next sc, dc in next sc**, ch 4, sc in next ch sp, ch 4, dc in next sc, rep from * across, ending last rep at **, turn. *(5 sc, 24 dc)*

Row 27: Ch 1, sc in each of first 4 dc, [ch 8, sc in each of next 4 dc] across, turn. *(24 sc)*

Row 28: Ch 3, dc in each of next 3 sc, *ch 4, sc in next ch sp, ch 4, dc in each of next 4 sc, rep from * across, turn. *(5 sc, 24 dc)*

Row 29: Ch 1, sc in each of first 4 dc, [ch 9, sc in each of next 4 dc] across, turn. *(24 sc)*

Row 30: Ch 3, dc in each of next 3 sc, [ch 5, sc in next ch sp, ch 5, dc in each of next 4 sc] across, turn. *(5 sc, 24 dc)*

Row 31: Ch 1, sc in each of first 4 dc, [ch 10, sc in each of next 4 dc] across, turn. *(24 sc)*

Row 32: Ch 3, dc in each of next 3 sc, [ch 6, sc in next ch sp, ch 6, dc in each of next 4 sc] across, turn to work in ends of rows. *(5 sc, 24 dc)*

JOINING TO BLANKET STITCHES
Holding pieces with WS tog and working in blanket stitches and ends of rows, ch 1, sl st in first blanket st, ch 2, sl st in first row, evenly sp [ch 1, sl st in next blanket st, ch 2, sl st in next row] across Pleat. Fasten off.

POCKET LINING
Row 1: On RS in upper row of stitching, join with sc in first double running stitch, [ch 1, sc in next double running st] across, turn.

Row 2: Ch 1, sc in first sc, [ch 1, sc in next sc] across, turn.

Rows 3–20: [Rep row 2] 18 times. At end of last row, fasten off.

POCKET WELT
Row 1: On RS in lower row of stitching, join with sc in first double running stitch, [ch 1, sc in next double running st] across, turn.

Row 2: Ch 1, sc in first sc, [ch 1, sc in next sc] across, turn.

Rows 3–9: [Rep row 2] 7 times. At end of last row, fasten off.

SLEEVE CUFFS
Rnd 1: With WS facing, join with sc in first blanket stitch, evenly sp [ch 1, sc in next blanket st] around, ch 1, **join** (see Pattern Notes) in beg sc, **turn**.

Rnd 2: Ch 1, sc in first sc, ch 1, [sc in next sc, ch 1] around, join in beg sc, turn.

Rnds 3–24: [Rep rnd 2] 22 times. At end of last rnd, fasten off.

Rep on rem Sleeve.

SLEEVE TRIM
With WS facing, join with sc in blanket stitch, ch 1, [sc in next blanket st, ch 1] around outer edges, join in beg sc. Fasten off.

FRONT OPENING AND LAPEL TRIM
Working in legs of blanket sts on WS of left front, join with sc in first blanket st, [ch 1, sc in next blanket st] across to shoulder seam. Fasten off.

Working in legs of blanket sts on WS of right front, join with sc in first blanket st at shoulder seam, [ch 1, sc in next blanket st] across to bottom. Fasten off.

TRIM
Row 1: With WS facing, join with sc in 4th sc of Lapel Trim before shoulder seam, [ch 1, sc in next sc] 3 times, [ch 1, sc in next blanket st] across neck line to next shoulder seam, [ch 1, sc in next sc] 4 times, turn.

Rnd 2: Ch 1, sc in first st, [ch 1, sc in next st] across neck line, working across front, back, pleats and front, evenly sp [ch 1, sc in next blanket st or st] around with evenly sp [ch 1, sc in next ch sp] around so piece lies flat, ch 1, join in beg sc. Fasten off.

FINISHING
Push pocket lining to inside and fold so last row meets lower row of double running stitches on WS. Using tapestry needle and yarn, sew in place and sew sides of pocket lining closed.

Fold pocket welt up. Using tapestry needle and yarn, sew sides to jacket front.

Center zipper over front trim below lapels as shown in photo. With sewing needle and thread, sew in place. ■

Stitch Guide

For more complete information, visit **FreePatterns.com**

ABBREVIATIONS

beg	begin/begins/beginning
bpdc	back post double crochet
bpsc	back post single crochet
bptr	back post treble crochet
CC	contrasting color
ch(s)	chain(s)
ch-	refers to chain or space previously made (e.g., ch-1 space)
ch sp(s)	chain space(s)
cl(s)	cluster(s)
cm	centimeter(s)
dc	double crochet (singular/plural)
dc dec	double crochet 2 or more stitches together, as indicated
dec	decrease/decreases/decreasing
dtr	double treble crochet
ext	extended
fpdc	front post double crochet
fpsc	front post single crochet
fptr	front post treble crochet
g	gram(s)
hdc	half double crochet
hdc dec	half double crochet 2 or more stitches together, as indicated
inc	increase/increases/increasing
lp(s)	loop(s)
MC	main color
mm	millimeter(s)
oz	ounce(s)
pc	popcorn(s)
rem	remain/remains/remaining
rep(s)	repeat(s)
rnd(s)	round(s)
RS	right side
sc	single crochet (singular/plural)
sc dec	single crochet 2 or more stitches together, as indicated
sk	skip/skipped/skipping
sl st(s)	slip stitch(es)
sp(s)	space/spaces/spaced
st(s)	stitch(es)
tog	together
tr	treble crochet
trtr	triple treble
WS	wrong side
yd(s)	yard(s)
yo	yarn over

Chain—ch: Yo, pull through lp on hook.

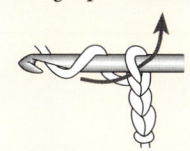

Slip stitch—sl st: Insert hook in st, pull through both lps on hook.

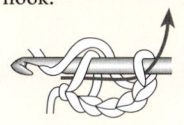

Single crochet—sc: Insert hook in st, yo, pull through st, yo, pull through both lps on hook.

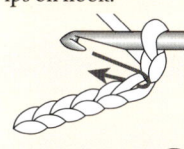

Front post stitch—fp:
Back post stitch—bp: When working post st, insert hook from right to left around post st on previous row.

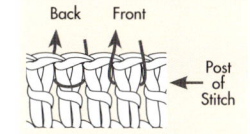

Front loop—front lp
Back loop—back lp

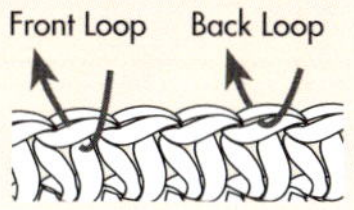

Half double crochet—hdc: Yo, insert hook in st, yo, pull through st, yo, pull through all 3 lps on hook.

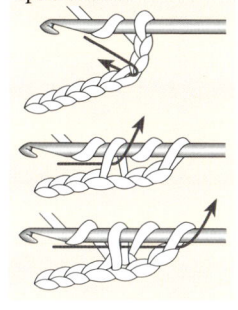

Double crochet—dc: Yo, insert hook in st, yo, pull through st, [yo, pull through 2 lps] twice.

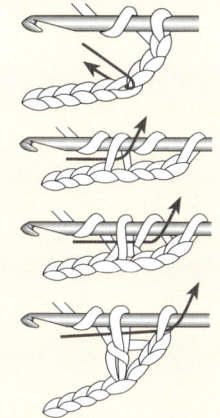

Change colors: Drop first color; with 2nd color, pull through last 2 lps of st.

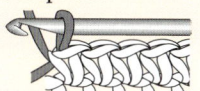

Treble crochet—tr: Yo twice, insert hook in st, yo, pull through st, [yo, pull through 2 lps] 3 times.

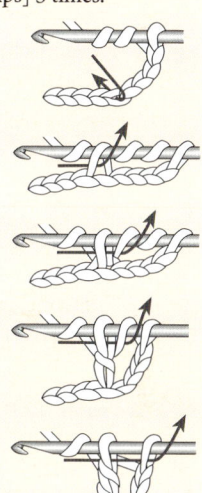

Double treble crochet—dtr: Yo 3 times, insert hook in st, yo, pull through st, [yo, pull through 2 lps] 4 times.

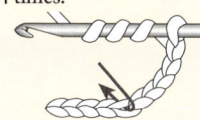

Single crochet decrease (sc dec): (Insert hook, yo, draw lp through) in each of the sts indicated, yo, draw through all lps on hook.

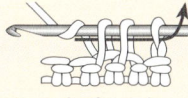

Example of 2-sc dec

Half double crochet decrease (hdc dec): (Yo, insert hook, yo, draw lp through) in each of the sts indicated, yo, draw through all lps on hook.

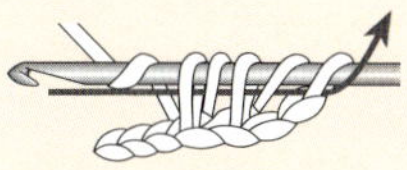

Example of 2-hdc dec

Double crochet decrease (dc dec): (Yo, insert hook, yo, draw loop through, draw through 2 lps on hook) in each of the sts indicated, yo, draw through all lps on hook.

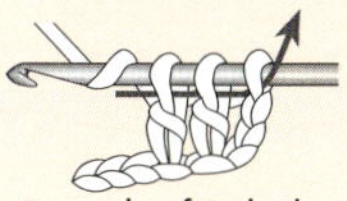

Example of 2-dc dec

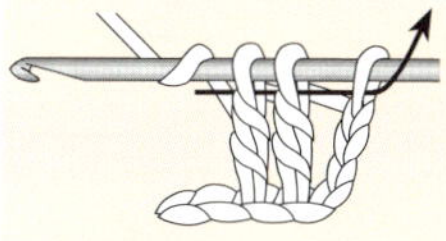

Treble crochet decrease (tr dec): Holding back last lp of each st, tr in each of the sts indicated, yo, pull through all lps on hook.

Example of 2-tr dec

US		UK
sl st (slip stitch)	=	sc (single crochet)
sc (single crochet)	=	dc (double crochet)
hdc (half double crochet)	=	htr (half treble crochet)
dc (double crochet)	=	tr (treble crochet)
tr (treble crochet)	=	dtr (double treble crochet)
dtr (double treble crochet)	=	ttr (triple treble crochet)
skip	=	miss

Metric Conversion Charts

METRIC CONVERSIONS

yards	x	.9144	=	metres (m)
yards	x	91.44	=	centimetres (cm)
inches	x	2.54	=	centimetres (cm)
inches	x	25.40	=	millimetres (mm)
inches	x	.0254	=	metres (m)

centimetres	x	.3937	=	inches
metres	x	1.0936	=	yards

INCHES INTO MILLIMETRES & CENTIMETRES (Rounded off slightly)

inches	mm	cm	inches	cm	inches	cm	inches	cm
1/8	3	0.3	5	12.5	21	53.5	38	96.5
1/4	6	0.6	5 1/2	14	22	56	39	99
3/8	10	1	6	15	23	58.5	40	101.5
1/2	13	1.3	7	18	24	61	41	104
5/8	15	1.5	8	20.5	25	63.5	42	106.5
3/4	20	2	9	23	26	66	43	109
7/8	22	2.2	10	25.5	27	68.5	44	112
1	25	2.5	11	28	28	71	45	114.5
1 1/4	32	3.2	12	30.5	29	73.5	46	117
1 1/2	38	3.8	13	33	30	76	47	119.5
1 3/4	45	4.5	14	35.5	31	79	48	122
2	50	5	15	38	32	81.5	49	124.5
2 1/2	65	6.5	16	40.5	33	84	50	127
3	75	7.5	17	43	34	86.5		
3 1/2	90	9	18	46	35	89		
4	100	10	19	48.5	36	91.5		
4 1/2	115	11.5	20	51	37	94		

KNITTING NEEDLES CONVERSION CHART

Canada/U.S.	0	1	2	3	4	5	6	7	8	9	10	10 1/2	11	13	15
Metric (mm)	2	2 1/4	2 3/4	3 1/4	3 1/2	3 3/4	4	4 1/2	5	5 1/2	6	6 1/2	8	9	10

CROCHET HOOKS CONVERSION CHART

Canada/U.S.	1/B	2/C	3/D	4/E	5/F	6/G	8/H	9/I	10/J	10 1/2/K	N
Metric (mm)	2.25	2.75	3.25	3.5	3.75	4.25	5	5.5	6	6.5	9.0

Annie's Attic®

Copyright © 2009 DRG, 306 East Parr Road, Berne, IN 46711. All rights reserved.
This publication may not be reproduced in part or in whole without written permission from the publisher.

TOLL-FREE ORDER LINE or to request a free catalog (800) LV-ANNIE (800) 582-6643
Customer Service (800) AT-ANNIE (800) 282-6643, **Fax** (800) 882-6643
Visit AnniesAttic.com
We have made every effort to ensure the accuracy and completeness of these instructions.
We cannot, however, be responsible for human error, typographical mistakes or variations in individual work.

ISBN: 978-1-59635-259-9

Printed in USA